In the Arms of God

In the Arms of God

DR. JAMES DOBSON

Tyndale House Publishers, Inc.
Wheaton, Illinois

Visit Tyndale's exciting Web site at www.tyndale.com

Quotations from Dr. James Dobson compiled by Sarah Peterson,
previously published in *When God Doesn't Make Sense*.

Cover photo by Gary Irving. All rights reserved.
Photography credits:
Christopher Talbot Frank: 3, 7, 17, 18, 21, 23, 31, 35, 39, 43, 45, 53, 57, 63, 75, 89, 91, 103, 105, 107, 111, 112, 115, 123, 126, 133, 149; Dennis Frates: 8, 11, 13, 26, 29, 47, 50, 55, 61, 65, 67, 70, 79, 80, 85, 87, 93, 97, 101, 121, 129, 135, 141; Gary Irving: 25, 33, 37, 59, 70, 77, 83, 117, 125, 131, 139, 143, 144, 147; Brian Eterno: 118.
Cover and interior design by Andrea Gjeldum.

ISBN 0-8423-1826-7

02 01 00 99 98
 6   5   4   3   2

CONTENTS

Part

ONE

God Is There

*E*ven when life does not make sense,

God has not lost control of our lives.

He wants us to trust Him.

His presence is very near.

But the eyes of the LORD are on those who fear him, on those whose hope is in his unfailing love. PSALM 33:18

IF YOU ARE
CONSIDERING GIVING UP
ON LIFE . . . THAT'S
PRECISELY WHAT

STRE

SATAN WOULD HAVE YOU DO:
GIVE UP ON GOD, WHO
SEEMS TO HAVE LOST
CONTROL OF YOUR
CIRCUMSTANCES. BUT GOD
KNOWS WHAT HE'S DOING;
DON'T LEAVE HIS
PROTECTION.

NGTH

God is our refuge and strength, a very present help in trouble. Psalm 46:1, KJV

*E*STABLISH YOUR FOUNDATION

NOT ON FLUCTUATING EMOTIONS

BUT ON THE AUTHORITY

OF THE WRITTEN WORD OF GOD.

IT SAYS JESUS PROMISED

NEVER TO LEAVE US.

---

*Go therefore and make disciples. . . . teaching them
to observe all things that I have commanded you;
and lo, I am with you always, even to the end of the
age. Amen.* MATTHEW 28:19-20, NKJV

WHEN YOUR FAITH IS SEVERELY SHAKEN, WHERE DO YOU GO TO FIND A NEW SET OF VALUES AND BELIEFS? WHILE SEARCHING FOR SOMETHING MORE RELIABLE IN WHICH TO BELIEVE, YOU WILL DISCOVER THAT THERE IS NO OTHER NAME—NO OTHER GOD—TO WHOM YOU CAN TURN.

"Though the mountains be shaken and the hills be removed, yet my unfailing love for you will not be shaken nor my covenant of peace be removed," says the LORD, who has compassion on you.

ISAIAH 54:10

$\mathcal{W}$E ARE PROMISED THROUGHOUT

SCRIPTURE THAT WE ARE NEVER LEFT TO

FIGHT OUR BATTLES ALONE.

THAT IS GREAT NEWS FOR ALL

WHO ARE WEARY AND BURDENED

BY THE STRESSES OF LIVING.

Therefore, having been justified by faith, we have peace with God through our Lord Jesus Christ. ROMANS 5:1, NKJV

CHRIST REMAINS WITH US

TO COMFORT AND PROTECT US WHEN

WE GO THROUGH OUR FIERY TRIALS.

HE NEVER LEAVES.

As the mountains surround Jerusalem, so the LORD surrounds his people both now and forevermore. PSALM 125:2

Part
_____
TWO

God Loves You

$\mathcal{G}$OD'S GREAT LOVE LED HIM

TO SEND HIS ONLY BEGOTTEN SON

AS A SACRIFICE FOR OUR SIN,

THAT WE MIGHT ESCAPE

THE PUNISHMENT WE DESERVE.

HE DID THIS BECAUSE

HE LOVES US.

---

*For God so loved the world, that he gave his only
begotten Son, that whosoever believeth in him should
not perish, but have everlasting life.* JOHN 3:16, KJV

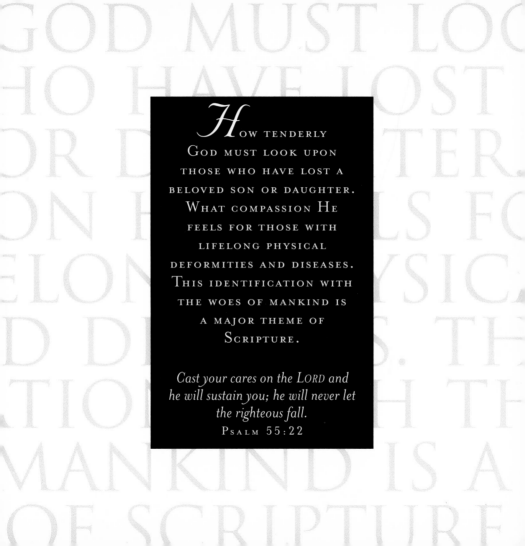

*H*OW TENDERLY
GOD MUST LOOK UPON
THOSE WHO HAVE LOST A
BELOVED SON OR DAUGHTER.
WHAT COMPASSION HE
FEELS FOR THOSE WITH
LIFELONG PHYSICAL
DEFORMITIES AND DISEASES.
THIS IDENTIFICATION WITH
THE WOES OF MANKIND IS
A MAJOR THEME OF
SCRIPTURE.

*Cast your cares on the LORD and
he will sustain you; he will never let
the righteous fall.*
PSALM 55:22

$\mathcal{I}$N GOD'S VALUE SYSTEM

WE ARE ALL IMPORTANT.

HE LOVES EVERY ONE

OF US THE SAME.

No longer will they call you Deserted, or name your land Desolate . . . for the LORD will take delight in you. ISAIAH 62:4

ONE OF THE MOST

BREATHTAKING CONCEPTS IN ALL

OF SCRIPTURE IS THE REVELATION

THAT GOD KNOWS EACH OF US PERSONALLY

AND THAT WE ARE IN HIS MIND

BOTH DAY AND NIGHT.

What is man that you are mindful of him, the son of man that you care for him?
PSALM 8:4

$\mathcal{T}$HERE IS SIMPLY NO WAY
TO COMPREHEND THE FULL
IMPLICATIONS OF THE LOVE
THE KING OF KINGS
AND LORD OF LORDS
HAS FOR US.

O LORD, You have searched me and known me. You know my sitting down and my rising up; You understand my thought afar off. PSALM 139:1-2, NKJV

$\mathcal{G}$OD CONTINUES

TO LOVE US—EVEN

WHEN WE ARE

ANGRY AT HIM.

Give thanks to the LORD,
for he is good; his love
endures forever.
PSALM 107:1

$\mathcal{N}$EVER ASSUME

GOD'S SILENCE

OR APPARENT INACTIVITY

IS EVIDENCE OF

HIS DISINTEREST.

Wait on the LORD, and keep his way, and he shall exalt thee to inherit the land: when the wicked are cut off, thou shalt see it. PSALM 37:34, KJV

$\mathcal{A}$DMITTEDLY, THE LORD DOESN'T ALWAYS SOLVE OUR PROBLEMS INSTANTANEOUSLY, AND HE SOMETIMES PERMITS US TO WALK THROUGH THE VALLEY OF THE SHADOW OF DEATH. BUT HE IS THERE WITH US EVEN IN THE DARKEST HOURS, AND WE CAN NEVER ESCAPE HIS ENCOMPASSING LOVE.

Yet I am always with you; you hold me by my right hand. PSALM 73:23

$\mathcal{E}$VERY DESCRIPTION GIVEN

TO US IN SCRIPTURE

DEPICTS GOD AS INFINITELY

LOVING AND KIND,

TENDERLY WATCHING OVER

HIS EARTHLY CHILDREN

AND GUIDING THE STEPS

OF THE FAITHFUL.

Come, let us bow down in worship, let us kneel before the LORD our Maker; for he is our God and we are the people of his pasture, the flock under his care. PSALM 95:6-7

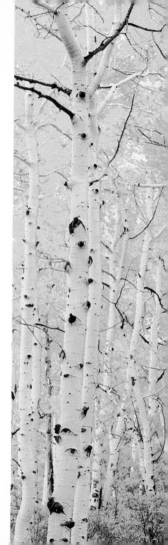

$\mathcal{G}$OD HEARS THE FAINTEST CRY

OF THE SICK, THE LONELY,

THE DESPISED OF THE WORLD.

AND HE CARES—DEEPLY—

ABOUT EACH ONE.

I waited patiently for the LORD; and he inclined unto me, and heard my cry. PSALM 40:1, KJV

$\mathcal{G}$OD'S HEART IS

ESPECIALLY TENDER TOWARD

THE DOWNTRODDEN

AND THE DEFEATED.

HE KNOWS YOUR NAME

AND HE HAS SEEN EVERY TEAR

YOU HAVE SHED.

The LORD is close to the brokenhearted and saves those who are crushed in spirit. PSALM 34:18

WHO CAN KNOW HOW OFTEN

THE LORD QUIETLY PROTECTS US,

REDIRECTS US, OR LEADS US

ON SAFER PATHS?

To man belong the plans of the heart, but from the LORD comes the reply of the tongue. PROVERBS 16:1

*H*ERE ARE THE TYPICAL COMPONENTS

OF A "FAITH UNDER FIRE": A VERY TROUBLING EVENT,

AN ELEMENT OF INJUSTICE OR UNFAIRNESS (WHY ME?),

A SILENT GOD WHO COULD HAVE INTERVENED BUT

DIDN'T, AND A MILLION UNANSWERED QUESTIONS.

HAVE YOU EVER BEEN THERE?

When the Chief Shepherd appears, you will receive the crown of glory that will never fade away. 1 PETER 5:4

SOMETIMES THE LORD

OFFERS NO EXPLANATION OR

INTERPRETATION OF HIS RESPONSE

TO OUR REQUESTS AND CRIES,

EXCEPT BY INFERENCE,

"THIS IS MY WILL FOR YOU."

The LORD is good to those who wait for Him, to the soul who seeks Him.
LAMENTATIONS 3:25, NKJV

*T*HERE ARE PURPOSES THAT YOU

CANNOT PERCEIVE OR COMPREHEND.

YOU MAY NEVER UNDERSTAND—

AT LEAST NOT IN THIS LIFE—BUT

YOU MUST NEVER LET GO

OF YOUR FAITH.

Now faith is being sure of what we hope for and certain of what we do not see. HEBREWS 11:1

THE LAWS OF
PHYSICS TELL US
THAT ENERGY IN

And we, who with unveiled faces all reflect the Lord's glory,
with ever-increasing glory, which comes

THE UNIVERSE
IS NEVER LOST.
IT IS SIMPLY
TRANSFORMED
FROM ONE STATE
TO ANOTHER. SO
IT IS WITH HUMAN
EXPERIENCE.
NOTHING IS EVER
LOST ENTIRELY.
GOD USES
EVERY
HAPPENING

TO
ACCOMPLISH
HIS DIVINE
PURPOSES.

are being transformed into his likeness

from the Lord, who is the Spirit. 2 CORINTHIANS 3:18

*W*HEN WE SUBMIT OURSELVES TO THE SOVEREIGN WILL OF THE LORD, WE CAN SAY WITH CONFIDENCE THAT IN ALL THINGS—YES, IN ALL THINGS—GOD WORKS FOR THE GOOD OF THEM WHO LOVE HIM, WHO HAVE BEEN CALLED ACCORDING TO HIS PURPOSE.

Every good gift and every perfect gift is from above, and comes down from the Father of lights, with whom there is no variation or shadow of turning.

JAMES 1:17, NKJV

$\mathcal{R}$EV. REUBIN WELCH,

MINISTER AND AUTHOR,

ONCE SAID, "WITH GOD,

EVEN WHEN NOTHING IS HAPPENING

—SOMETHING IS HAPPENING."

IT IS TRUE.

I wait for the LORD, my soul doth wait, and in his word do I hope.
PSALM 130:5, KJV

SCRIPTURE TELLS US

THAT WE LACK THE CAPACITY

TO GRASP GOD'S INFINITE MIND

OR THE WAY HE INTERVENES

IN OUR LIVES.

The secret things belong to the LORD our God, but the things revealed belong to us and to our children forever, that we may follow all the words of this law. DEUTERONOMY 29:29

JEHOVAH DIDN'T EXPLAIN TO JOSEPH WHAT

HE WAS DOING THROUGH YEARS OF HEARTACHE

(HE WAS HATED BY HIS BROTHERS, SOLD AS A SLAVE,

IMPRISONED, FALSELY ACCUSED OF ATTEMPTED RAPE,

THREATENED WITH EXECUTION). HE WAS EXPECTED,

LIKE YOU AND ME, TO LIVE OUT EACH DAY

IN SOMETHING LESS THAN

COMPLETE UNDERSTANDING.

"For my thoughts are not your thoughts, neither are your ways my ways,"
declares the LORD. ISAIAH 55:8

$\mathcal{W}$E CAN SAY WITH CONFIDENCE THAT WHILE GOD'S PURPOSES AND PLANS ARE VERY DIFFERENT FROM OURS, HE IS INFINITELY JUST AND HIS TIMING IS ALWAYS PERFECT.

O Sovereign LORD, you are God! Your words are trustworthy, and you have promised these good things to your servant. Now be pleased to bless the house of your servant, that it may continue forever in your sight; for you, O Sovereign LORD, have spoken, and with your blessing the house of your servant will be blessed forever. 2 SAMUEL 7:28-29

*I*F HUMAN INTELLIGENCE

AND PERCEPTION ARE UNDEPENDABLE

IN ASSESSING EVERYDAY REALITY,

WHICH CAN BE SEEN, TOUCHED, HEARD,

TASTED, AND SMELLED,

HOW MUCH LESS CAPABLE ARE THEY

OF EVALUATING THE UNFATHOMABLE

GOD OF THE UNIVERSE?

So we fix our eyes not on what is seen, but on what is unseen. For what is seen is temporary, but what is unseen is eternal. 2 CORINTHIANS 4:18

SOONER OR LATER OUR INTELLECT WILL POSE QUESTIONS WE CANNOT POSSIBLY ANSWER. AT THAT POINT, WE WOULD BE WISE TO REMEMBER GOD'S WAYS ARE HIGHER THAN OURS.

Then my soul will rejoice in the LORD and delight in his salvation. My whole being will exclaim, "Who is like you, O LORD? You rescue the poor from those too strong for them, the poor and needy from those who rob them." PSALM 35:9-10

ONE OF THE GREATEST
DESTROYERS OF FAITH
IS TIMING THAT DOESN'T FIT
OUR PRECONCEIVED NOTIONS.
WE LIVE IN A FAST-PACED WORLD
WHERE WE HAVE COME TO EXPECT
INSTANT RESPONSES TO EVERY
DESIRE AND NEED. BUT GOD
DOESN'T OPERATE THAT WAY.
HE IS NEVER IN A HURRY.

And he said unto them, "It is not for you to know the times or the seasons, which the Father hath put in his own power." ACTS 1:7, KJV

*E*ven Jesus, who lived thirty-three years on earth, spent only three in active ministry! Think of how many more people He could have healed—and how many more divine truths He could have imparted—in another decade or two. But He, too, ministered according to God's schedule.

To every thing there is a season, and a time to every purpose under the heaven: A time to be born, and a time to die; a time to plant, and a time to pluck up that which is planted. Ecclesiastes 3:1-2, kjv

Growth through Trials

GOD WILL CO

TO USE YOUR

AND NER

ABO OUR

NCE STR

AIT OTH

ARE SUFFERI

ND FEELING

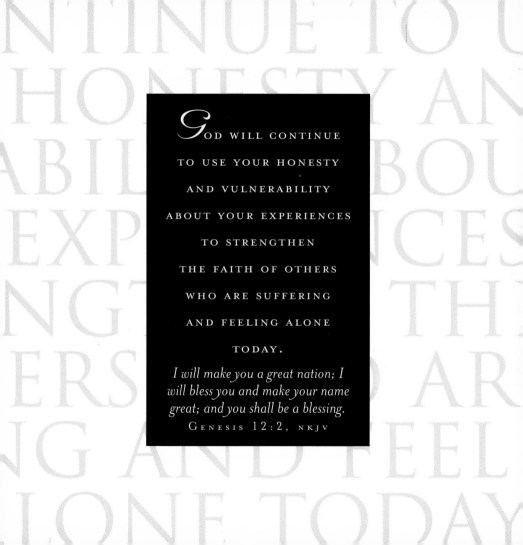

*G*OD WILL CONTINUE
TO USE YOUR HONESTY
AND VULNERABILITY
ABOUT YOUR EXPERIENCES
TO STRENGTHEN
THE FAITH OF OTHERS
WHO ARE SUFFERING
AND FEELING ALONE
TODAY.

*I will make you a great nation; I
will bless you and make your name
great; and you shall be a blessing.*
GENESIS 12:2, NKJV

I

LET GOD BE GOD.
THEREIN LIES THE
SECRET TO THE
"PEACE THAT
TRANSCENDS
UNDERSTANDING."

God said to Moses, "I AM WHO I AM. This is what you are to

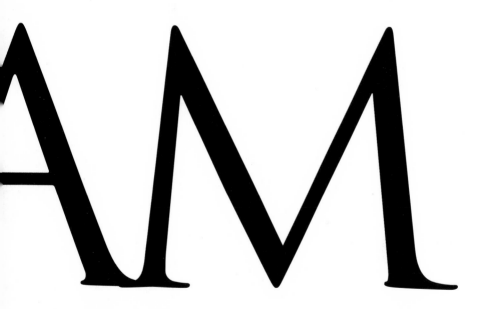

say to the Israelites: 'I AM has sent me to you.'" Exodus 3:14

$\mathcal{M}$OST BELIEVERS ARE PERMITTED TO GO THROUGH EMOTIONAL AND SPIRITUAL VALLEYS THAT ARE DESIGNED TO TEST THEIR FAITH IN THE CRUCIBLE OF FIRE. WHY? BECAUSE FAITH RANKS AT THE TOP OF GOD'S SYSTEM OF PRIORITIES.

And without faith it is impossible to please God, because anyone who comes to him must believe that he exists and that he rewards those who earnestly seek him. HEBREWS 11:6

*R*OCK-SOLID FAITH IN GOD

WILL HOLD YOU WHEN

YOU WALK THROUGH THE VALLEY

OF THE SHADOW OF DEATH,

BECAUSE YOU NEED FEAR NO EVIL.

LIFE CAN NEVER TAKE YOU

BY SURPRISE AGAIN.

But the Lord is faithful, who shall stablish you, and keep you from evil.
2 THESSALONIANS 3:3, KJV

$\mathcal{I}$ AM CONVINCED THAT THE

HEART OF THE LORD IS DRAWN

TO THOSE WHO HOLD FAST TO THEIR

FAITH IN TIMES OF DESPAIR.

Draw nigh to God, and he will draw nigh to you.
Cleanse your hands, ye sinners; and purify your
hearts, ye double-minded. JAMES 4:8, KJV

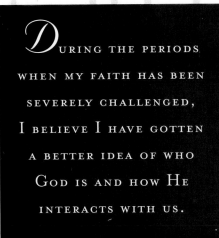

*D*URING THE PERIODS
WHEN MY FAITH HAS BEEN
SEVERELY CHALLENGED,
I BELIEVE I HAVE GOTTEN
A BETTER IDEA OF WHO
GOD IS AND HOW HE
INTERACTS WITH US.

*He will cover you with his feathers,
and under his wings you will find
refuge; his faithfulness will be your
shield and rampart.*
PSALM 91:4

*J*ESUS CHRIST HAS PROMISED TO

TAKE OUR HARDSHIPS AND BRING

GOOD FROM THEM.

But from everlasting to everlasting the LORD's love is with those who fear him, and his righteousness with their children's children—with those who keep his covenant and remember to obey his precepts. PSALM 103:17-18

*A*LL OF THE BIBLICAL

WRITERS, INCLUDING THE GIANTS

OF THE FAITH, WENT THROUGH

HARDSHIPS.

Blessed is every one that feareth the Lord; that walketh in his ways. For thou shalt eat the labour of thine hands: happy shalt thou be, and it shall be well with thee. PSALM 128:1-2, KJV

*P*AIN AND SUFFERING DO NOT CAUSE

THE GREATEST DAMAGE IN TIMES OF TRIAL.

CONFUSION IS THE FACTOR THAT

SHREDS ONE'S FAITH.

Blessed be the God and Father of our Lord Jesus Christ, who according to His abundant mercy has begotten us again to a living hope through the resurrection of Jesus Christ from the dead, to an inheritance incorruptible and undefiled and that does not fade away, reserved in heaven for you. 1 PETER 1:3-4, NKJV

$\mathcal{S}$OMETIMES GOD LETS
YOU AND ME STRUGGLE UNTIL WE
RECOGNIZE OUR DEPENDENCE ON
HIM. IN SO DOING, HE GIVES
OUR FAITH AN OPPORTUNITY TO
GROW AND MATURE.

I pray that you, being rooted and established in love, may have power, together with all the saints, to grasp how wide and long and high and deep is the love of Christ, and to know this love that surpasses knowledge—that you may be filled to the measure of all the fullness of God. EPHESIANS 3:17-19

*A*RE WE DESTINED TO BE

DEPRESSED AND VICTIMIZED BY

THE CIRCUMSTANCES OF OUR LIVES?

CERTAINLY NOT.

THE APOSTLE PAUL SAID WE ARE

"MORE THAN CONQUERORS"

—AND THAT WE ARE!

Therefore he is able to save completely those who come to God through him, because he always lives to intercede for them. HEBREWS 7:25

THE CHRISTIAN LIFE

IS A COEXISTENCE OF BOTH

JOY AND PAIN.

Thou shalt also be a crown of glory in the hand of the LORD, and a royal diadem in the hand of thy God. ISAIAH 62:3, KJV

Part
FIVE

Forgiveness to Acceptance

*W*HAT ADVICE IS AVAILABLE FOR
THAT INDIVIDUAL WHO IS BITTER AND DEEPLY ANGRY
AT GOD FOR SOME PERCEIVED MISDEED?
THERE IS ONLY ONE CURE FOR THE CANCER OF
BITTERNESS: TO FORGIVE THE PERCEIVED OFFENDER,
ONCE AND FOR ALL, WITH GOD'S HELP.

If we confess our sins, he is faithful and just and will forgive us our sins and purify us from all unrighteousness. 1 JOHN 1:9

Trust in the LORD *with all thine heart and lean not on thine own*

understanding. PSALM 46:1

RESENTMENT AND BITTERNESS CAN BE CLEANSED. THERE IS NO BETTER WAY TO GET RID OF THEM THAN TO ABSOLVE THE LORD OF WHATEVER WE HAVE HARBORED, AND THEN ASK HIS FORGIVENESS FOR OUR LACK OF FAITH. THIS RECONCILIATION IS THE ONLY WAY YOU WILL ENTIRELY BE FREE.

SOME OF US NEED TO FORGIVE
GOD FOR HEARTACHES THAT ARE
CHARGED TO HIS ACCOUNT.
IF YOU'VE CARRIED RESENTMENT
AGAINST HIM FOR YEARS,
LET GO OF IT.

You are a forgiving God, gracious and compassionate, slow to anger and abounding in love. NEHEMIAH 9:17

*H*OW WRONG IT IS

TO PLACE THE BLAME FOR YOUR TROUBLES

ON THE BEST FRIEND MANKIND EVER HAD!

REGARDLESS OF OTHER CONCLUSIONS

YOU DRAW, PLEASE BELIEVE THIS:

GOD IS NOT THE SOURCE OF YOUR PAIN!

For if, when we were God's enemies, we were reconciled to him through the death of his Son, how much more, having been reconciled, shall we be saved through his life! Not only is this so, but we also rejoice in God through our Lord Jesus Christ, through whom we have now received reconciliation. ROMANS 5:10-11

$\mathcal{M}$OST OF US STRUGGLE TO

"BE ANXIOUS FOR NOTHING" WHEN

WE ARE AGITATED OR FRIGHTENED

BY EVENTS IN OUR LIVES.

STILL, WE CAN LEARN TO

LET GOD BE GOD AND ACCEPT HIS

DIRECTION AND JUDGMENT.

Commit thy works unto the LORD, and thy thoughts shall be established. PROVERBS 16:3, KJV

*I*F WE TRULY UNDERSTOOD THE MAJESTY

OF THE LORD AND THE DEPTH OF HIS LOVE FOR US,

WE WOULD CERTAINLY ACCEPT THOSE TIMES

WHEN HE DEFIES HUMAN LOGIC AND SENSIBILITIES.

INDEED, THAT IS WHAT WE MUST DO.

For the LORD God is a sun and shield: the LORD will give grace and glory: no good thing will he withhold from them that walk uprightly. PSALM 84:11, KJV

Part
SIX

Peace and Hope

$\mathcal{B}$ECAUSE OF THE REDEEMER,

WE NEED NOT FEAR

THE GREAT DECEIVER—THE

FATHER OF LIES.

My sheep listen to my voice; I know them, and they follow me. I give them eternal life, and they shall never perish; no one can snatch them out of my hand. My Father, who has given them to me, is greater than all; no one can snatch them out of my Father's hand. JOHN 10:27-29

A BETTER DAY IS
COMING FOR THOSE
WHOSE SOURCE OF
CONTENTMENT IS
IN THE PERSONHOOD
OF CHRIST JESUS!

*Blessed are the pure in heart,
For they shall see God.*
MATTHEW 5:8, NKJV

*O*UR JOY AND OUR HOPE

CAN BE AS STEADY AS THE SUNRISE

EVEN WHEN THE HAPPENINGS AROUND

US ARE TRANSITIONING FROM

WONDERFUL TO TRAGIC.

They that sow in tears shall reap in joy. He that goeth forth and weepeth, bearing precious seed, shall doubtless come again with rejoicing, bringing his sheaves with him. PSALM 126:5-6, KJV

*T*HERE IS SECURITY AND REST

IN THE WISDOM OF THE ETERNAL

SCRIPTURES.

If any of you lacks wisdom, let him ask of God, who gives to all liberally and without reproach, and it will be given to him. JAMES 1:5, NKJV

P R

Devote yourselves to *prayer, being*

watchful and thankful. Colossians 4:2

Our foundation as believers is rooted in Scripture, which was "God-breathed" and then dutifully recorded by inspired writers of the Word. Its message is unmistakable: that in all circumstances we should pray and give thanks.

*T*HE HOPE OF CHRIST'S

RETURN BURNS WITHIN MY BREAST.

IT IS THE ULTIMATE ANSWER TO

THOSE WHO SUFFER AND

STRUGGLE TODAY.

For what is our hope, our joy, or the crown in which we will glory in the presence of our Lord Jesus when he comes? Is it not you? Indeed, you are our glory and joy. 1 THESSALONIANS 2:19

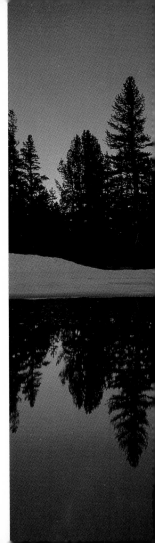

$\mathcal{K}$NOW THE LORD IS

IN CONTROL, AND REFUSE TO BE

SHAKEN IN YOUR FAITH.

For God did not give us a spirit of timidity, but a spirit of power, of love and of self-discipline.
2 TIMOTHY 1:7

SCRIPTURE TELLS US TO EXPECT SUFFERING AND HARDSHIP, YET ENCOURAGES US TO BE THANKFUL AND "OF GOOD CHEER." HOW CAN WE BE TRIUMPHANT AND UNDER INTENSE PRESSURE AT THE SAME TIME? THAT IS A MYSTERY THAT "TRANSCENDS ALL UNDERSTANDING." BUT PEACE IS AVAILABLE—EVEN IN TIMES OF STORM.

Blessed be God, even the Father of our Lord Jesus Christ, the Father of mercies, and the God of all comfort; Who comforteth us in all our tribulation, that we may be able to comfort them which are in any trouble, by the comfort wherewith we ourselves are comforted of God. 2 CORINTHIANS 1:3-4, KJV

I MAY LACK THE WORDS
TO DESCRIBE WHAT OCCURS
TO THE FAITHFUL IN TIMES
OF PERSONAL CRISIS. LET
IT BE SAID, SIMPLY, THAT
THERE IS OFTEN A QUIET
AWARENESS IN THE MIDST
OF CHAOS THAT THE LORD
IS THERE AND HE IS STILL
IN CONTROL.

*If you love Me, keep My command-
ments. And I will pray the Father,
and He will give you another
Helper, that He may abide with
you forever—the Spirit of truth.*
JOHN 14:15-17, NKJV

$\mathcal{G}$OD'S PEACE

IS ALWAYS THERE FOR THOSE WHO

CHOOSE TO TAKE IT.

Blessed are the peacemakers, for they shall be called sons of God. MATTHEW 5:9, NKJV

CHRISTIANS WHO LOSE GOD
DURING A PERIOD OF SPIRITUAL CONFUSION
ARE LIKE A VINE CUT OFF FROM ITS SOURCE.
DEPRIVED OF NURTURE AND STRENGTH,
THEY COPE AT FIRST, BUT SOON BEGIN
TO WITHER. THEY DROP OUT OF CHURCH
AND QUIT READING THE BIBLE AND PRAYING.
WHAT THEY DON'T REALIZE IS THAT,
WITHOUT GOD, THERE'S NO PEACE WITHIN.

I am the vine; you are the branches. If a man remains in me and I in him, he will bear much fruit; apart fom me you can do nothing. JOHN 15:5

*L*ET GOD BE GOD.

THEREIN LIES THE SECRET TO THE

"PEACE THAT TRANSCENDS

UNDERSTANDING."

May God himself, the God of peace, sanctify you through and through. May your whole spirit, soul and body be kept blameless at the coming of our Lord Jesus Christ. The one who calls you is faithful and he will do it.
1 THESSALONIANS 5:23-24

*I*F YOU COULD FULLY

COMPREHEND HOW DEEPLY

YOU ARE LOVED BY GOD,

YOU WOULD NEVER FEEL

ALONE AGAIN.

For as the heaven is high above the earth, so great is his mercy toward them that fear him. PSALM 103:11, KJV

Part

SEVEN

Building Faith and Trust

OUR TASK IS NOT TO DECIPHER

EXACTLY HOW ALL OF LIFE'S PIECES

FIT AND WHAT IT ALL MEANS, BUT TO

REMAIN FAITHFUL AND OBEDIENT TO

HIM WHO KNOWS ALL MYSTERIES.

*Dear friends, now we are children of God, and
what we will be has not yet been made known. But
we know that when he appears, we shall be like him,
for we shall see him as he is.* 1 JOHN 3:2